GW00372962

Living Corals
© 2001 Times Media Private Limited
Reprinted 1987, 1991, 1997, 2001

Les Editions du Pacifique
An imprint of Times Media Private Limited
A member of the Times Publishing Group
Times Centre
1 New Industrial Road, Singapore 536196
Tel: (65) 2848844 Fax: (65) 2854871
E-mail: te@tpl.com.sg
Online bookstore: http://www.timesone.com.sg/te

Typeset in France by Compographic
Printed in Malaysia

All rights reserved for all countries

ISBN: 981-204-775-1

Living corals

Text: B. ROBIN
Photography: C. PETRON · C. RIVES
Translated by: B. PICTON (Ulster Museum, Belfast)

LES·EDITIONS·DU·PACIFIQUE

contents

Introduction

One of the most spectacular events of our time has been the discovery of the underwater world of the tropics. It is another universe, extensively photographed and filmed, in which the coral scenery forms a backdrop to the numerous brightly-coloured reef fishes which generate as much interest as the most famous actors. The best opportunity to observe the mysterious lives of these creatures is presented to the scuba diver, but in the midst of this enchanting coral scenery he can become like a visitor to an art gallery without a catalogue. The works can be admired but the artists and their subjects remain a complete mystery.

The aim of this book, therefore, is to increase the knowledge of this coral universe, and to make visitors to the tropical seas not be content merely with trips in glass-bottomed boats but to encourage them to don mask, snorkel and fins and discover at close range these animals whose beauty is unmatched by anything on dry land.

To complete this short preamble we must express our gratitude to M. Percier, director of the Museum of the Sea at Biarritz and to Dr. J-P. Chevalier of the National Museum of Natural History in Paris, both of whom have shown unlimited patience and devotion in giving us the benefit of their advice.

A small group of fishes swimming above a forest of Acropora. *At the least sign of danger they will take refuge in the shelter of the coral branches.*

Classification

The corals are among the simplest of forms of marine life and belong to a branch of the cœlenterates. This name is derived from the Greek word « Cœlenteron » (hollow-gut) which represents their common characteristic ; they always have a hollow pocket which carries out most physiological functions. The cœlentrates are one of the most diverse and important groups of animals to be found in the sea. The group includes many organisms which superficially appear very different to the sculptured, mineral-like corals. Sea anemones appear to be elegant plant-forms and in the jellyfish the animal is soft, translucent and fragile, like an enormous caricature of the first attempts at life.

Thus in this one group of animals nature seems to display her three kingdoms, animal, vegetable and mineral. However, these apparent divergences are reconciled when we see how a number of corals are the most perfect examples of a harmony which intimately links these animals with complex physio-chemical

This mushroom of dead, fossilised coral implanted in the reef platform provides evidence of the sea level at the beginning of the quaternary era.

reactions to plants and minerals.

Before getting down to the details of classification it must be admitted that the definition of the word coral is very imprecise, and different authors do not always accept the same limits so that what is a coral to one is certainly not to another. The name first arose when applied to a particular species, *Corallium rubrum,* the precious red coral. In the course of time the meaning of the word has changed, and now it encompasses numerous groups of animals which by their anatomical, biological and evolutionary characteristics are sometimes only distantly related to each other. It is these characters which separate the corals thriving in a few

metres of well-oxygenated, warm, sunlit water in the tropics from their fellows which live under the enormous pressure of kilometres of water in the perpetually dark, cold waters of the abyss.

To help clarify the situation it is useful to set out the groups in a simple, schematic system. The Phylum

The fishes in this picture look like they are about to have dinner ! A beautiful colony of Acropora *in the form of an inverted umbrella provides the table, while to the left a colony of* Porites *resembles a velvet cushion. On the floor the carpet is formed by the white coral sand of the lagoon. This is a typical underwater scene on a barrier reef in 1 to 3 metres of water.*

Cœlenterata may be divided into two subphyla :-
− The **Cnidaria** which have stinging cells. (We shall be dealing only with this group).
− The **Ctenophora** which have no stinging cells.

The **Cnidaria** are divided into three super-classes :
− The **Anthozoa** and the **Hydrozoa** which we will discuss further.
− The **Scyphozoa** which are types of jellyfish such as the Portuguese Man-of-War. They are often found washed up on beaches : none of them are corals.

The super-class **Hydrozoa** will only detain us briefly as corals are only found in one of its four constituent orders ; the **Hydrocorallia**. On the other hand the superclass **Anthozoa** requires detailed examination as it contains a number of coral types. This group is divided into two classes depending on the number of radial partitions found in the polyps :

− eight partitions and eight tentacles characterise the class **Octocorallia**.

− six partitions or tentacles (or multiples of six) characterise the class **Hexacorallia** which contains the great majority of the splendid corals responsible for the fabulous underwater scenery of tropical seas.

Of all these levels of classification it is, however, only really a knowledge of the classes which is important. The class to which a particular species belongs depends on the basic number of subdivisions of the gut-cavity of the polyp. Whether the mode of life is solitary or colonial, whether or not a skeleton exists and

The reef untiringly rebuilds itself, the corals interweave with one another and are cemented together by calcareous algae which ensure a strong construction. Below surface reflections a colony of Acropora *and two small growths of* Porites *bring new life to the dead coral on which they are growing.*

PRINCIPAL CORALS

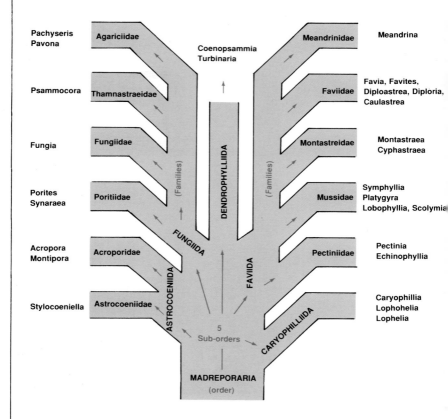

SUB-ORDERS, FAMILIES, AND GENERA OF THE MADREPORARIA WHICH ARE MENTIONED MOST OFTEN IN THE TEXT OF THIS BOOK. (N.B. a number of families and genera are not included in this diagram).

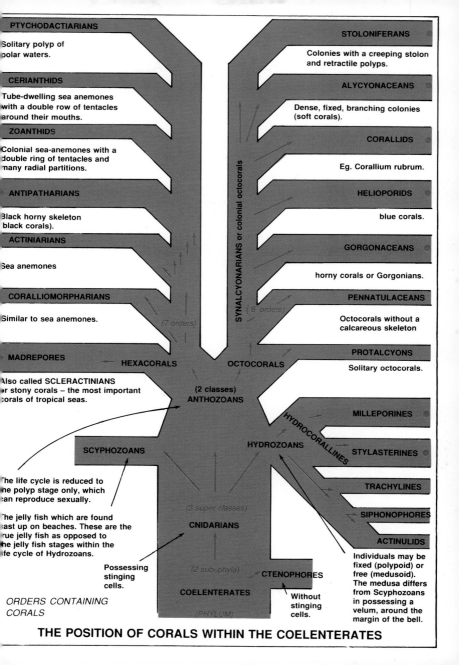

PTYCHODACTIARIANS

Solitary polyp of polar waters.

CERIANTHIDS

Tube-dwelling sea anemones with a double row of tentacles around their mouths.

ZOANTHIDS

Colonial sea-anemones with a double ring of tentacles and many radial partitions.

ANTIPATHARIANS

Black horny skeleton (black corals).

ACTINIARIANS

Sea anemones

CORALLIOMORPHARIANS

Similar to sea anemones.

MADREPORES

Also called SCLERACTINIANS or stony corals – the most important corals of tropical seas.

HEXACORALS

(7 orders)

(2 classes)
ANTHOZOANS

STOLONIFERANS

Colonies with a creeping stolon and retractile polyps.

ALYCYONACEANS

Dense, fixed, branching colonies (soft corals).

CORALLIDS

Eg. Corallium rubrum.

HELIOPORIDS

blue corals.

GORGONACEANS

horny corals or Gorgonians.

PENNATULACEANS

Octocorals without a calcareous skeleton

PROTALCYONS

Solitary octocorals.

SYNALCYONARIANS or colonial octocorals

(6 orders)

OCTOCORALS

SCYPHOZOANS

The life cycle is reduced to the polyp stage only, which can reproduce sexually.

The jelly fish which are found cast up on beaches. These are the true jelly fish as opposed to the jelly fish stages within the life cycle of Hydrozoans.

HYDROZOANS

HYDROCORALLINES

MILLEPORINES

STYLASTERINES

TRACHYLINES

SIPHONOPHORES

ACTINULIDS

Individuals may be fixed (polypoid) or free (medusoid). The medusa differs from Scyphozoans in possessing a velum, around the margin of the bell.

(3 super classes)

CNIDARIANS

Possessing stinging cells.

(2 sub-phyla)

CTENOPHORES

Without stinging cells.

COELENTERATES

(PHYLUM)

ORDERS CONTAINING CORALS

THE POSITION OF CORALS WITHIN THE COELENTERATES

if so, whether it is horny or strongly calcified. From this level onwards the classification leads into orders, sub-orders and families, but rather than pursue these more and more detailed divisions the reader is presented here with a simplified account. Another drawback with the finer divisions of the classification is that the terminology varies from author to author, one man's family may be another's order !

A disadvantage of only looking at the classification on such a large scale is that it has prevented us from doing justice to the **Madreporaria,** the stony corals, which is the main order of corals in the **Hexacorallia.** This group alone makes up virtually all of the bulk of the coral world, including such enormous and impressive coral formations as the Great Barrier Reef of Australia, the Maldives Archipelago in the Indian Ocean, and the Tuamotu reefs of the Pacific. Nevertheless this colossal mass of living material which has formed such a volume of rock is only a fraction of the total achievement of Madrepore corals. These reefs are in geological terms only of recent formation, only a few thousand years old. Where then are the results of the unceasing growth of Madrepore corals for the last 100 million years ? This group appeared at the beginning of the Triassic era, and benefitting from constant changes of climate and water levels caused by the movements of the Earth's continents, they have adapted to the confusion of geological upheavals and, at one time or another, have built their reefs over pratically the whole of the globe. They surrounded islands of past eras with huge barrier reefs which are now mountains and uplands of limestone. Every country has examples ; the Burren in Ireland, the Mendip hills in England and the Massif Central of France. These are the ancient monuments of coral adaptation to the many migrations of the oceans this planet has known in the course of its evolution.

The natural history of true coral : the Madrepores.

As well as being marvels of the underwater world the corals are also marvels of anatomical and physiological organisation, making the polyp a masterpiece of miniaturisation. The natural history of coral may be better understood by first following the life-cycle.

After its release from the egg the coral larva must first survive dangerous wanderings in the open sea. It then becomes fixed to a suitable support and its development is controlled by inbuilt laws of organogenesis which have remained constant for thousands of years. These laws are different for each species, and govern the growth and organisation of both the soft parts and the remarkable architecture of the mineral skeleton. This association of fragile pinnacles stretches ever upwards and outwards to form robust fortresses with strong walls. Then we will see how the coral uses a weapon of diabolical cunning for feeding, defence and attack. Only the coelenterates possess this brilliant invention, which consists of a poisonous harpoon which may be compared with the curare-coated darts fired from the blow pipes of the Jivaro indians. Finally we will examine the way in which coral is able to face up to the enemies and forces which constantly threaten destruction, and how, to our great pleasure, the coral adorns itself with all the colours of the painter's palette. This gives the exterior of living coral the thousand fires of a precious stone when we see it under ultra-violet light.

The birth of a coral

The coral polyp results from the encounter of a spermatozooid with an egg cell, and as both of these

cells can be released from the rudimentary sexual glands within the mesenteries of a single polyp, the coral is considered to be a hermaphrodite.

After a few days in the shelter of the stomach cavity, which plays the protective role of the womb, the egg divides to become a tiny ciliated larva only two millimetres in lengh, called a planula. This larva is then expelled through the mouth opening of its parent polyp, and leaves the shelter of its early life. Extremely poorly protected from a multiple of dangers it is thrown into the ocean. As if drawn towards the new protection of

These constantly changing light patterns are characteristic of coral scenery near to the surface. Over the sand to the right and on the mass of Porites *in the foreground the suns rays are transformed into luminous waves by the surface ripples.*

the warmth of the sun, the planula immediately swims towards the surface to live as part of the great body of zooplankton. The endless movements of the currents may carry the planula far away. Whatever its birthplace, whether on the exposed edge of the fore-reef or within the shelter of a lagoon, sooner or later the larva is forced to wander aimlessly by the sea currents. Many larvae are swept out into the infinity of the open Ocean and may be lost forever from the propagation of the species. The harsh law of selection is merciless, even though they turn their carnivorous tendencies against other members of the zooplankton, they are just as likely to be eaten themselves by a larger carnivore whose staple diet is the zooplankton itself.

In normal circumstances this free-floating stage of the life cycle only lasts a few days. At the end of their planktonic life the planulae settle to the sea bed and begin to search for a suitable solid support to which they can attach themselves for the rest of their days.

Coral growth and development

A complete description of the organogenesis of the polyp and of its complex morphology is beyond the scope and intent of this book. Nevertheless it will be useful to describe the organisation of an adult polyp, using as an example a **madrepore**. We will look at the soft parts in the order of their development from the planula as well as how the skeleton is built by the soft body for its support and protection. We must never lose sight, however, of the fact that these two elements of the polyp have evolved as a unit, and are not independent of one another.

Once fixed to its support, the larva begins a series of changes leading to the adult form, which is a solitary polyp whose size may be anything from a few millimetres to several centimetres. At first it looks like a little vase, the opening of which will be the mouth, the neck will be a sort of œsophagus called the stomodeum while the body, evenly inflated, will be the gastro-vascular cavity. Within this space vertical partitions called mesenteries grow out from the walls towards the centre. These mesenteries do not unite in the centre of the cavity but divide it into a series of chambers. They are grouped in pairs, and in the **Hexacorallia** they are present in multiples of six.

Around the edge of the mouth the animal bears tentacles which are arranged in concentric rings, or cycles. The soft parts of the polyp are basically constructed of three layers. Derived from these layers are a number of specialised cells which may almost be considered as organs.

The outer layers is the ectoderm. This is the sensitive skin of the polyp and tentacles. It contains six different types of cell, the most important of which are

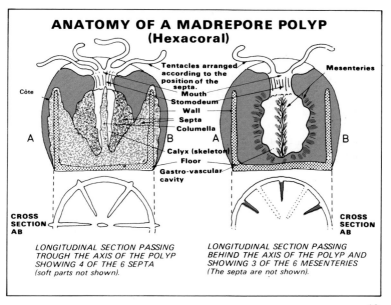

ANATOMY OF A MADREPORE POLYP
(Hexacoral)

Tentacles arranged according to the position of the septa.

Mesenteries

Côte

Mouth
Stomodeum
Wall
Septa
Columella

Calyx (skeleton)
Floor
Gastro-vascular cavity

A   B   A   B

CROSS SECTION AB

CROSS SECTION AB

LONGITUDINAL SECTION PASSING TROUGH THE AXIS OF THE POLYP SHOWING 4 OF THE 6 SEPTA (soft parts not shown).

LONGITUDINAL SECTION PASSING BEHIND THE AXIS OF THE POLYP AND SHOWING 3 OF THE 6 MESENTERIES (The septa are not shown).

the cnidoblasts or stinging cells. (These are the cells common to all members of the sublphylum **Cnidaria**). The cnidoblast is an ingenious weapon, used both for defence and attack. The surface of the tentacles is packed with batteries of these cells which are a combination of a speargun and a hypodermic syringe. Each cell has a trigger, a harpoon attached by a line, and a spring. The line is hollow and delivers an injection of poison under pressure after the harpoon penetrates. By stretching time and space we can describe the melodrama which occurs in a few thousandths of a second and in the space of fifty microns of cnidoblast when a planktonic organism triggers the cnidocil. The capsule lid flies open and the liquid inside is suddenly relieved of pressure, forcing out the stinging filament. The filament is inverted, like the finger of a rubber glove turned inside out, and unrolls inside itself as the glove does when you blow into it. Barbs on the inside of the tube swing round to the outside and tear a hole in the victim, and the filament enters this hole to inject a charge of venom. Having completed this job the cnidoblast cannot be reloaded. It dies and is cast off to be replaced by another cell from below, which rapidly differentiates into an identical cnidoblast.

The internal layer is the endoderm. This lines the gastrovascular cavity of the polyp and forms a vast surface for digestion on the many folds of the mesenteries. This layer is mainly responsible for digestion, and consists of many glandular cells which produce digestive enzymes, surrounded by a network of muscle fibres.

Between the endoderm and the ectoderm is the mesogloea. This layer is not composed of cells, but is secreted by the other two layers. It performs the function of the connective tissues of higher animals. It is a transparent gelatine-like sustance, and embedded

ANATOMY OF THE CNIDOBLAST
(contained in the ectoderm of the polyp)

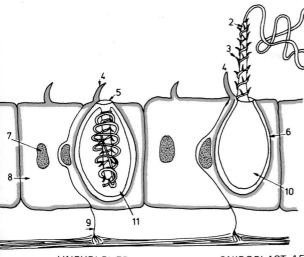

1. Stinging Filament
2. Tube
3. Spines
4. Cnidocil
5. Operculum
6. Cnidocyst
7. Cell nucleus
8. Ectodermal cell
9. Nerve Fibre
10. Cnidoblast cavity empty of poison
11. Poison under pressure

UNEXPLOVED CNIDOBLAST

CNIDOBLAST AFTER EJECTION OF THE FILAMENT

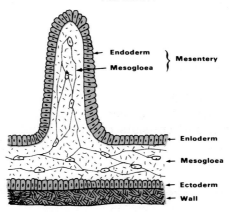

DIAGRAM SHOWING THE 3 CELL LAYERS OF THE SOFT TISSUES
(Each is represented, somewhat artificially, as being only a single cell thick).

in it are the masses of reproductive cells which form rudimentary testes and ovaries.

Even as these specialised tissues are being formed the ectoderm becomes active to build for the polyp its marvellous skeleton. First it must build a solid foundation. At the periphery of the pedal disc a calcareous deposit is laid down in the form of a ring. This enlarges into a continuous disc which anchors the polyp firmly to its support.

As soon as the foundations of the edifice are secure building can commence. A circular enclosing wall is built vertically like a castle around the edge of the fixation zone. This eventually becomes a cylindrical calcareous structure called a Calyx. To reinforce this wall the polyp architect also erects six vertical lamellae which act like flying buttresses, and are called septa. The upper edges of these septa are free at the top of the calyx and so provide the decorative patterns : smooth and sharp, stout, toothed, wavy, etc. The polyp never ceases in its work of reinforcing the tower it has constructed. Between the six primary septa it builds six more septa, not quite as stout as the first (second order septa). In the twelve spaces thus created it may build twelve more, even thinner, third order septa. The number of septa is always related to the number of mesenteries and the number of tentacles which the polyp possesses, and it may go on adding cycles of septa as it grows, the final pattern being characteristic of each species.

We must now examine the building material used by the polyp. Within the ectodermal layer there are special cells called calicoblasts, whose function is to produce the building blocks of the structure by secreting calcium carbonate in the form of the crystal Aragonite. One of the secrets of the construction is that the calicoblasts are prismatic cells, two microns thick by

MORPHOLOGY OF THE CALYX
of a hexacoral

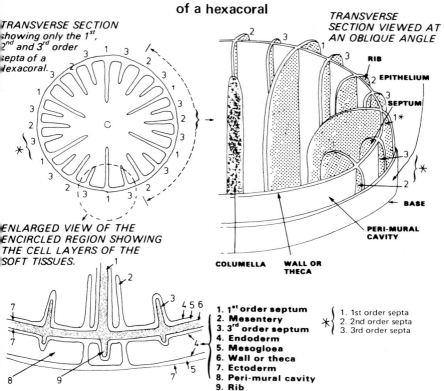

TRANSVERSE SECTION showing only the 1st, 2nd and 3rd order septa of a hexacoral.

TRANSVERSE SECTION VIEWED AT AN OBLIQUE ANGLE

RIB
EPITHELIUM
SEPTUM
BASE
PERI-MURAL CAVITY
COLUMELLA
WALL OR THECA

ENLARGED VIEW OF THE ENCIRCLED REGION SHOWING THE CELL LAYERS OF THE SOFT TISSUES.

1. 1st order septum
2. Mesentery
3. 3rd order septum
4. Endoderm
5. Mesogloea
6. Wall or theca
7. Ectoderm
8. Peri-mural cavity
9. Rib

* 1. 1st order septa
  2. 2nd order septa
  3. 3rd order septa

THE TWO PRINCIPAL METHODS OF SKELETAL CONSTRUCTION USED BY THE POLYP TO AVOID STRETCHING THE SOFT TISSUES AS THE CALYX GROWS IN HEIGHT

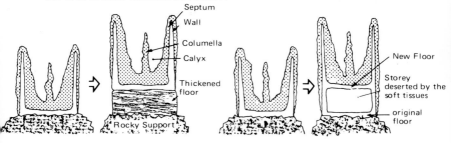

Septum
Wall
Columella
Calyx
Thickened floor
Rocky Support

New Floor
Storey deserted by the soft tissues
original floor

THICKENING OF THE ORIGINAL FLOOR.　　2. CONSTRUCTION OF A NEW FLOOR

ten microns wide and long. This explains the regular shape of the bricks used for building the structure.

The polyp therefore becomes the owner of a fine castle, strengthened with cross walls and buttresses. The vertical growth of the walls and septa continues to deepen the calyx, which eventually becomes too long for the soft body of the polyp within it. At this stage the polyp again displays its talents as an architect and builds a transverse calcareous floor across the calyx, thus permitting occupation of only the upper storey of its tower, and abandoning the lower part completely. According to the whim of the architect the floors may be a simple thickening of the foundation disc, which results in a gradual rise of the base of the calyx, or horizontal shelves welded at their edges to the sides, leaving the lower floor hollow and empty.

Thus lodged on the top floor of a fortified tower which it periodically but tirelessly builds upwards, the polyp is able to ornament its house with rocky flourishes characteristic of its species. These decorations include a columella which is a calcareous column occupying the vertical axis of the calyx, and elongation of the septa beyond the lateral walls.

We must now consider the mysterious events involving animal and mineral, which have, over the aeons of geological time, resulted in the construction of large sections of continents. It may be useful to compare the construction of the calcareous skeleton of the polyps with the process of bone formation in mammals. For its construction, bone requires a basic framework on which deposition of calcium carbonate from the blood can take place. The coral also constructs an organic matrix to begin with, which then serves as a mould for deposition of the calcium carbonate. The calcium comes from the body fluids of the polyp, which is similar in constitution to sea-water, but also similar to blood-plasma. Analogies such as these bring us a little closer to understanding how the polyp constructs its skeleton. The major role is played by the microscopic chemical factory located in the calicoblast cytoplasm, where a molecular precursor is synthesised. This molecule is then attached to the cell membrane of the endoderm cell, where it modifies the physio-chemical properties of the membrane and enables selective absorption of calcium and carbonate ions from the sea water. The combination of these ions results in the formation of the Aragonite crystalline form of Calcium carbonate. This crystallisation is quite different to mere precipitation of lime, as it is mediated and controlled by the enzyme carbonic anhydrase which is synthesised by the polyp.

The polyp skeleton therefore, as in oyster shells, mother of pearl, and pearls themselves, is contructed of a calcified organic compound, superior to the basic mineral in strength and consistency. Moreover it is the organic matrix which determines the pattern of calcification, controlling its everchanging shape to produce the coral skeleton and eventually the entire coral reef.

The corals way of life and its struggle for survival

Despite the protection of its skeletal armour, the polyp is still a fragile organism which must use all the tricks of its trade to survive. In some species the polyp remains solitary and may reach a size of several centimetres in diameter, other species have very small polyps which must form a colony to enable them to survive and compete.

For successful growth the coral requires certain conditions of water clarity, temperature and salinity, without which life is terminated by a sort of wasting away. In order to survive the polyp must carry out all the major functions of animal life successfully, complying with the restrictions and requirements placed upon it by the environment. We will examine these requirements and the polyps ways of coping with them in this chapter.

When the first polyp of a colonial coral has reached maturity the animal begins to form a colony by a second type of reproduction called budding. This budding is an asexual form of reproduction, and may be intra − or extra − calical.

In the case of intracalical budding the bud is formed at the oral disc, which elongates and then pinches off in the middle, giving two individuals which remain joined at the base and by part of their gastro-vascular cavity, like siamese twins.

Alternatively in the case of extracalical budding the polyp gives rise to a small polyp by growth from an evagination of part of the soft parts of the original polyp. The new bud begins immediately to secrete its own skeleton alongside its parent polyp.

Colonies increase in size by one or other of these types of budding, giving rise to the many forms which make up the great diversity of coral reefs found all over the tropical world. Only in the thermal conditions, salinity, water clarity, light intensity and oxygenation

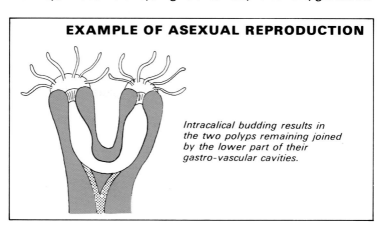

EXAMPLE OF ASEXUAL REPRODUCTION

Intracalical budding results in the two polyps remaining joined by the lower part of their gastro-vascular cavities.

state found in the reef communities can the coral carry out these major life functions.

Having looked at growth and the two types of reproduction , sexual and asexual, only the nutrition of the polyp remains to be discussed.

Corals are carnivorous, and like the big cats, hunt mainly at night. Because of their small size their normal prey is zooplankton, which may include small crustaceans and larvae of larger animals. It is well-known that the plankton layers tend to migrate nearer to the surface at night, and therefore it is at dusk that the polyp begins to hunt. The soft parts, retracted by day into their calyces, expand, the tentacles extend and wave about, blindly exploring the surrounding water with that delicate sensitivity bestowed by blindness. This demonstrates the perfect coordination established between the muscle cells, sensory cells and nerve net of the polyp. Observation of the polyp as it slowly emerges from its calyx, expanding and dilating its body and tentacles, enables us to appreciate these cellular interactions. Similarly to see the retreat into the calyx, in a fraction of a second, caused by the slightest alarm gives us an indication that the coordination and speed involved in these responses must require a large number of nerve cells cooperating in the role of a spinal cord.

During the polyps nocturnal hunting it is sufficient for the tentacles only to gently touch the prey to cause an immediate firing of a battery of poisonous harpoons from the cnidoblasts. The prey, entangled and paralysed, is then drawn into a mass of writhing tentacles and conveyed gently but firmly to the mouth. Digestion occurs in the gastrovascular cavity, where the enzymes secreted by the endoderm rapidly break down the food into easily assimilable products.

A balanced diet, however, also requires sugars. To obtain these the corals have a particularly cunning arrangement, which is the main secret of their success in the clear tropical waters where plankton food is scarce and valuable. In the tissues of the polyps, and those of the larvae, are unicellular algae called zooxanthellae. These algae carry out photosynthesis, and using only sunlight, water and carbon dioxide they can produce the vital sugars which the polyp needs for energy and elaboration of its organic skeleton.

This symbiosis of polyp and zooxanthellae is the reason for the corals requirement for clear, brightly lit waters. The chloroplyll can only carry out its miracle of synthesis if it is provided with light energy. Our knowledge of photosynthesis also provides a clue to understanding how certain species of coral can flourish even at depths of fifty metres or more. There are, in fact, several types of Chlorophyll, and also other accessory pigments, which can capture not only the rapidly absorbed light near the surface but also the blue light which penetrates to these depths. Zooxanthellae possessing these pigments can provide their hosts with the necessary carbohydrates even in such dim light. This symbiosis is so vital to the corals, that we can consider the zooxanthellae as a virtual organ of the polyp, without which it could grow only extremely slowly, and create only a very fragile skeleton.

Further evidence for the importance of these plants to the coral is the fact that there is up to three times as much plant tissue as animal tissue in a coral colony.

Chorophyll not only possesses the fabulous chemical powers which enable life to continue both on land and in the sea, but it also contributes to the splendid colours of the reefs by mixing with yellow, blue, orange, violet, and brown pigments dispersed in the polyp in the form of tiny granules only 2 um in diameter. These tissue pigments are also responsible

Following page : in the foreground the outer slope of the reef is notched by deep gullies above which the waves are breaking. The waves die away as they enter the lagoon, whose shallow waters are pale turquoise. In the background is the island of Tahiti.

DIAGRAM OF THE NUTRITIONAL CYCLE

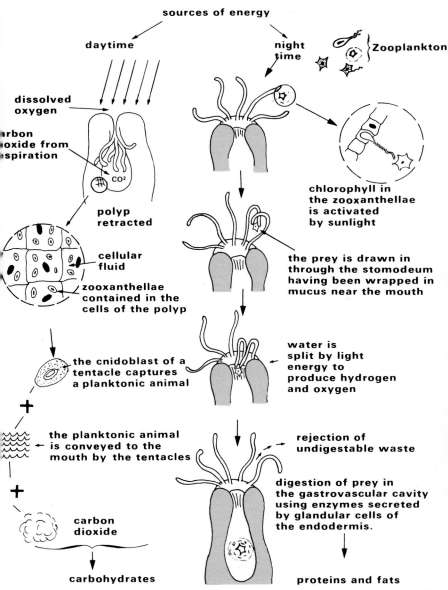

sources of energy

daytime

night time

Zooplankton

dissolved oxygen

carbon dioxide from respiration

CO^2

polyp retracted

cellular fluid

zooxanthellae contained in the cells of the polyp

chlorophyll in the zooxanthellae is activated by sunlight

the prey is drawn in through the stomodeum having been wrapped in mucus near the mouth

the cnidoblast of a tentacle captures a planktonic animal

water is split by light energy to produce hydrogen and oxygen

+

the planktonic animal is conveyed to the mouth by the tentacles

rejection of undigestable waste

digestion of prey in the gastrovascular cavity using enzymes secreted by glandular cells of the endodermis.

+

carbon dioxide

carbohydrates

proteins and fats

for the magnificent phenomenon of fluorescence exhibited by the corals apparently for our pleasure. Rays of ultraviolet light, which are invisible to our eyes, are converted by these pigments to green, orange, blue or red light, giving great beauty to the masses of tentacles and transforming them into glinting emeralds, rubies or sapphires.

The inhabitants of the coral

In the tangled underwater jungle of the coral reef the branching thickets of coral provide a protective refuge for a great variety of marine animals.

The best known are the damsel fishes (*Chromis* and *Dascyllus*) which live at the very base of the clumps of *Acropora.* They do not risk hunting in open water unless they are certain there are no predators about, and even then they dash back to their shelters at the least disturbance. There, they are so sure of their invulnerability that nothing will dislodge them. The same attachment to these branching homes is shown by certain gobies, and by *Caracanthus* which can wedge themselves in place amongst the coral branches by means of spines on their gill covers.

Along with these fish, crabs of the genus *Porcellana* and many brittle stars also live amongst the *Acropora* branches. The female of the crab *Mapalocarcinus* goes even further in obtaining protection by living imprisoned in a coral outgrowth, rather like a gall, which she creates for herself. Thus condemned to the life of a recluse her only contact with the water outside is by means of holes in her chamber which she herself maintains. Through these holes comes food-bearing water and also visiting male crabs, which are very small and can slip through the bars of her prison.

The relationship between the coral and its lodgers must pose problems of good neighbourliness. Why for instance are the *Chromis* not stung by the thousands of cnidoblasts on the corals tentacles, which constantly brush them when the polyps are expanded ? Perhaps they are protected by the same mechanism as the clown fishes (*Amphiprion*) which live amongst the stinging tentacles of large sea anemones.

The enemies of the coral

To counteract this coral animal which seems capable of spreading indefinitely nature has assigned a battery of destructive forces. The methods of adaptation of corals to hot sunshine, powerful waves, storms and coatings of sand vary from species to species and affect the position of individual species in the ecological arrangement of the reefs. During low spring tides corals living near the surface may be exposed to strong sunlight which can be deadly. Certain species therefore, and in particular *Porites,* have acquired resistance to this dessication by secreting copious amounts of mucus. Corals growing at the exposed edge of a reef must withstand the constant battering of the waves and swell which continuously attempt to dislodge them. This requires such corals to construct solid foundations, massive formations and also to allow rapid repair work by the calcareous algae which cement together this part of the reef.

Coral must also avoid being buried by sand. Storms, currents and even Parrot-fish which grind living coral to sand with their massive teeth, give the reef a permanent showering of sediment of one type or another. Provided this coating is not too sudden or too dense the polyps can clean themselves by movements of their tentacles and by the action of the cilia which coat their bodies. Sudden burial under large amounts of sediment is bound to be fatal, as the polyps rapidly starve and asphyxiate.

Coral is also attacked by various predators. It is amazing that these mountains of organic material are not palatable to far more animals. The multitudes of fish which do feed on the coral must be armed to deal with the stony skeleton, and are immune to the cnidoblasts secreted poison.

Chaetodons or butterfly fish have long snouts drawn out like pipettes for capturing the tiny inhabitants of coral crevices, and can decapitate extended polyps. Parrot-fish and Trigger fish are not so concerned with devouring the soft parts exclusively, and browse on the branching extremities of the colonies with their powerful jaws and formidable rasp-like pharyngeal teeth. They swallow the entire coral, digesting the organic parts and depositing the powdered skeletal material as tiny clouds of sand over the coral meadows. While the coral extracts calcium from the sea-water these fish return it to the ocean in the form of pulverised lime which partly redissolves and partly remains as particles to re-enter the continuous sand cycle.

By far the most devastating predator of coral is the huge starfish *Acanthaster planci* (crown of thorns starfish) which is up to 60 centimetres in diameter and eats coral. While sitting on a coral outcrop it evaginates its stomach to surround the structure exactly and then dissolves the organic matter completely with digestive enzymes. After this onslaught the entire coral is dead and only a bare skeleton remains. Provided the natural balances are maintained *Acanthaster planci* is just another inhabitant of the reef, a zoological curiosity. However recently in some areas this balance seems to have been upset and vast plagues of these monsters have descended on the reefs and destroyed large areas of coral. This is thought to be possibly due to interference by man with the natural enemies of the

A splendid but destructive echinoderm, Acanthaster planci, *the crown of thorns starfish whose proliferation has caused the destruction of entire reefs.*

starfish, which normally keep its populations in check.

A few plants may be classed as enemies of the coral. Certain microscopic algae called *Trichodesmium* which are normal members of the phytoplankton may under certain circumstances produce such large blooms that the underlying coral is killed by the toxins they produce. This is very rare, however, and of far greater significance are the helpful calcareous algae such as *Porolithon onkodes* and *Porolithon gardineri.* These algae are important to the growth of the reef, as they cement together and strengthen the coral, especially at exposed parts of the reef where they compete in outward growth with the coral itself.

Sadly we must end this chapter with the greatest danger to the coral, which in the last few decades has caused great damage to these beautiful animals. It is sad because the cause of this destruction is the ignorance of man himself. Whenever we interfere in a coral reef area we can easily upset the delicate balance of nature and rapidly create an underwater desert. In many reef areas building has taken place on the atolls and the coral itself is used for making concrete. This stirs up clouds of dust and sand which settles in such vast amounts that the self-cleaning capacity of the polyps cannot cope.

Another much more serious threat is the film of oil which is now found along most of the world's shipping lanes. In these areas the spectacular coral beds, previously a fairyland, have become a nightmare of shapeless, colourless masses of the limestone, over which other more resistant but far less interesting organisms spread eagerly.

Other types of coral

Within the madrepore corals we have been describing there is great uniformity, allowing a general description of their way of life. These are the commonest corals in the tropics, and what variation there is forms the basis for their division into various classes and orders. This uniformity is not found in the many other types of coral which we will now consider, each group exhibits its own peculiarites.

For example, not all polyps reproduce in a hermaphrodite fashion as described above. In some species the male and female organs are found on different polyps of the same colony, in other species entire colonies are male or female and the sperm must swim through the open seas to find an egg and carry out fertilisation in the gastro-vascular cavity of another polyp. This last state of affairs is found in *Goniopora* for example. This may not be so different, as even in the hermaphrodites there must be a fair amount of cross fertilisation of colonies, in order to maintain the genetic variability of the species. However in *Millepora* which is a member of the super-class **Hydrozoa**, there is a free-living medusoid stage which swims in the plankton and produces the gametes. This is a totally different state of affairs to that found in the **Anthozoa**.

It is in the development and growth of these other corals, however, that the really big differences are found. There are a multitude of forms of anatomical organisation, and to appreciate these we will review the various types of coral. In the previous chapter we considered the unifying features of madrepore corals, but the morphological variations of the skeleton were not considered. In *Heliastraea* regularly-spaced circular

A gathering of giants. Solitary and freeliving, each of these Fungia *is a single polyp which has multiplied the number of septa in its skeleton almost infinitely, giving it a mushroom appearance.*

calyxes are formed, in *Favia* they are oblong and serrated, in *Platygyra* they are fused into channels, while in the **Faviidae** such as *Hydrophora* all of the calyxes are fused. (The reader will find examples of all these morphological variations in the photographic section of this book.)

As well as the colonial forms there are solitary corals which do not contribute greatly to the formation of the reef. These mostly live at depths between 25 and 40 metres, attached to broken coral fragments. The best examples of fluorescence are found among some of these species, which are only a solitary polyp with a single mouth, such as *Cynarina.* Some of these solitary corals, such as *Trachyphyllia* and especially *Fungia* live in only a few feet of water. *Fungia* is commonly called the mushroom coral, because of its radiating calcareous lamellae which make the skeleton look like an upturned, stalkless mushroom. This polyp is a giant amongst the corals, the skeleton may be up to twenty-five centimetres in diameter.

The method of budding in *Fungia* is equally unusual, an adult producing a kind of stalk which terminates in a tiny disc. This disc becomes a baby *Fungia* and begins to secrete its own skeleton. This baby is soon broken off from the « umbilical cord » which joins it to its mother, either by its own weight or by wave action in the shallow water where they live, and the young *Fungia* leaves to start its independent existence. Because its underside is concave and touches the substrate only at its edges, and because it is nearly weightless when buoyed up by the water around it, the polyp can move around, almost like a millipede, by using its tentacles and the cilia around its edges. Even more important in the shallow water is its ability to right itself if it falls face downwards in the sand. The tentacles are then capable of coordinated movement and extension to regain the correct position for feeding.

The Antipatharians or Black corals

The black corals, a favourite material for craftsmen in the Red Sea and Caribbean, belong to the order **Antipatharia** of the Class **Hexacorallia**. These colonial forms have minute polyps which are only visible under a microscope and possess six non-retractable tentacles. The skeleton is neither external, nor of lime. The colonies resemble the finest twigs of a tree, and their major constituent is a hard, black horny substance. The surface of these twigs is rough with minute spines. The soft parts of the colony are spread all over the outside of this axial skeleton in a thin film, rather like the bark of a tree. Black corals have no zooxanthellae and therefore no need for sunlight, they often live at great depths, from 30 metres to as deep as 2 500 metres where they have no competition from madrepore corals. The majority of species live in the tropics, but a few live in more temperate waters such as the Mediterranean *Parantipathe larix*.

The Octocorals – Red coral and Soft corals

The **Octocorals** are the second major class of corals. Several characters are common to all of the six orders which make up this class, and before describing the orders we will deal with these distinguishing characters of octocorals.

Octocorals are all colonial and have very small polyps, with the mouth surrounded by eight pinnate tentacles, that is to say the tentacles have tiny lateral branches or pinnules giving the whole structure a feather-like appearance. The pharynx is a longitudinal gutter connecting to the gastrovascular cavity, which is divided up by eight radial mesenteries. The calyx has eight corresponding septa. The skeleton is quite unlike that of the **Hexacorallia**, as it is usually constructed by

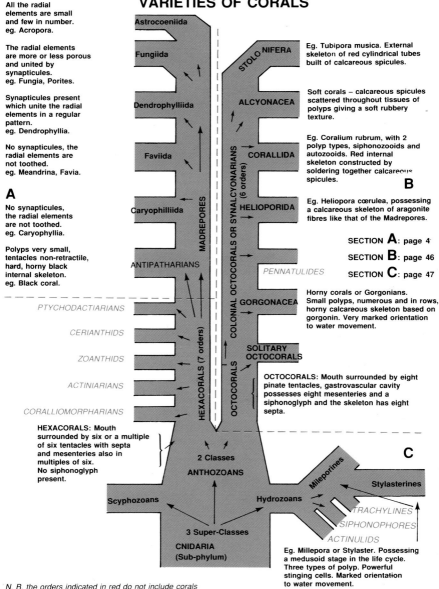

RECAPITULATORY TABLE OF THE PRINCIPAL CHARACTERISTICS OF DIFFERENT VARIETIES OF CORALS

All the radial elements are small and few in number. eg. Acropora.

The radial elements are more or less porous and united by synapticules. eg. Fungia, Porites.

Synapticules present which unite the radial elements in a regular pattern. eg. Dendrophyllia.

No synapticules, the radial elements are not toothed. eg. Meandrina, Favia.

A

No synapticules, the radial elements are not toothed. eg. Caryophyllia.

Polyps very small, tentacles non-retractile, hard, horny black internal skeleton. eg. Black coral.

Astrocoeniida

Fungiida

Dendrophylliida

Faviida

Caryophilliida

ANTIPATHARIANS

MADREPORES

PTYCHODACTIARIANS

CERIANTHIDS

ZOANTHIDS

ACTINIARIANS

CORALLIOMORPHARIANS

HEXACORALS (7 orders)

HEXACORALS: Mouth surrounded by six or a multiple of six tentacles with septa and mesenteries also in multiples of six. No siphonoglyph present.

STOLONIFERA

ALCYONACEA

CORALLIDA

HELIOPORIDA

PENNATULIDES

GORGONACEA

SOLITARY OCTOCORALS

COLONIAL OCTOCORALS OR SYNALCYONARIANS (6 orders)

OCTOCORALS

Eg. Tubipora musica. External skeleton of red cylindrical tubes built of calcareous spicules.

Soft corals – calcareous spicules scattered throughout tissues of polyps giving a soft rubbery texture.

Eg. Coralium rubrum, with 2 polyp types, siphonozooids and autozooids. Red internal skeleton constructed by soldering together calcareous spicules.

B

Eg. Heliopora cœrulea, possessing a calcareous skeleton of aragonite fibres like that of the Madrepores.

SECTION **A**: page 4
SECTION **B**: page 46
SECTION **C**: page 47

Horny corals or Gorgonians. Small polyps, numerous and in rows, horny calcareous skeleton based on gorgonin. Very marked orientation to water movement.

OCTOCORALS: Mouth surrounded by eight pinate tentacles, gastrovascular cavity possesses eight mesenteries and a siphonoglyph and the skeleton has eight septa.

C

2 Classes
ANTHOZOANS

Scyphozoans

Hydrozoans

Milleporines

Stylasterines

TRACHYLINES
SIPHONOPHORES
ACTINULIDS

3 Super-Classes
CNIDARIA
(Sub-phylum)

Eg. Millepora or Stylaster. Possessing a medusoid stage in the life cycle. Three types of polyp. Powerful stinging cells. Marked orientation to water movement.

N. B. the orders indicated in red do not include corals

ACROPORA
pages 82 à 92

FUNGIA
page 110

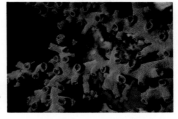

DENDROPHYLLIA
page 114

FAVIA
pages 116 à 118

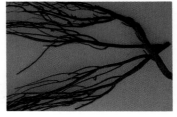

BLACK CORAL
page 134

TUBIPORA MUSICA
page 134

ALYCYONACEAN
pages 135 et 136

CORALLIUM RUBRUM
page 134

**HELIOPORA
COERULEA**

GORGONIAN
pages 134 à 136

ZOANTHID
page 136

ACTINARIAN

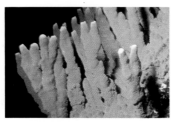

MILLEPORA
pages 138 à 140

DISTICHOPORA VIOLACEA

the scleroblasts which occur in the mesogloea. The skeleton is therefore internal and varies in constitution from group to group. It may consist of calcareous spicules either separate or welded together into a network, or of a horny protein material, or of amorphous lime, or various mixtures of these components. Our previous examination of the processes involved in construction of the inorganic skeleton of the madrepores indicates the complex biochemistry carried out by the scleroblasts. These cells of the **Octocorals** are far more versatile and change their function from one genus to another to a far greater extent than do the calicoblasts of the **madrepores**.

Having considered the unifying features of all Octocorals we must now look at the distinctive characters of the different orders.

The Corallidae – The most valuable and highly prized coral since the earliest times, the red coral, *Corallium rubrum,* is the most famous species belonging to this order. For the purists it is only this species which can really be called a coral, as it is the original owner of the name. Its colonies live only in deep water and dark places such as caves. In the Mediterranean drastic collecting has now confined it to depths of fifty metres or more, but it is also found in Japan and in the Antilles. The polyps are of two types, some are sterile and have no tentacles and seem to specialise in cleaning the colony. Others have tentacles for feeding and contain both the male and female gonads. The skeleton which is used for jewellery is internal, and owes its beautiful orange colour to the presence of iron salts.

A rocky tree built by an animal, might be a good description of this splendid growth of coral, perhaps a hundred years old. The little inhabitants of the reef become almost invisible when hidden amongst its branches.

The Stoloniferae – These are mostly small creeping octocorals but the order contains one species, *Tubipora,* which is most unique. The species *Tubipora musica* ta ressembles the pipes of a cathedral organ, the colony being made up of a series of cylindrical tubes of a lovely brick-red colour, joined together in places by horizontal struts.

The Heleporidae – This third order of corals possesses a few species which give the corals some of the most wonderful colours with which they grace the underwater scenery. *Helepora* is the only genus in the order and *Helepora caerulea* is the most spectacular species, commonly known as the blue coral. Its beautiful bright steely-blue colour is due to iron salts in its skeleton. This massive, colonial form is encountered in the reefs of the Indo-Pacific, and, as in the Madrepores, its skeleton is built up of calcium carbonate crystals.

The Alcyonidae – Scientists and naturalists are continuously arguing about the inclusion of this group under the name Corals. However coral is a very imprecise term and it seems sensible to include these genera. The term soft corals has widely been adopted in the tropics to distinguish these species from the Madrepores, and satisfies most of the specialists. These species freqently grow to considerable size, but have only a scattering of calcareous spicules which can scarcely be called a skeleton, their texture is rubbery. Some types are bush like, such as *Spongodes merleti* while others such as certain species of the genus *Sarcophyton* look more like giant mushrooms. Many species have beautiful colours, and they make a lovely contrast to the skeletal forms in reef areas. They are also masters of the phenomenon of fluorescence as many species of true corals.

The Gorgonidae – This is the final order of the **Octocorals,** and another group which many zoologists would not include under the term coral, but they are often called horny corals so we cannot ignore them completely. **Gorgonians** or Sea-fans are colonies of many rows of polyps arranged on a tree-like skeleton of a horny-calcareous, virtually unbreakable material. The basic substance of this skeleton is secreted by the endodermal cells and is known as gorgonin. The colonies can grow to an enormous size, in the Red Sea some species reach 2-5 metres across. They are found at all depths, and have an interesting habit. The colonies are always flattened in one plane. Near the surface they are arranged so that their branches are parallel to the surface but at depth they extend out vertically perpendicular to the face of the reef. The reason for this is to take advantage of water movement ; swell near the surface and currents at depth. The animals grow out in the direction which enables them to maximise the efficiency of collection of nocturnal plankton by the stinging tentacles of their polyps, placing their meshwork across the water movement like a net.

The Hydrocorallia – Fire Coral

To complete our review of corals we must briefly consider a **Cnidarian** from the other super-class, **the Hydrozoa.** This deserves the name coral far less than all the previously discussed species, but its common name, fire coral, given because of the painful smarting burns it produces on those foolish enough to brush against it, means that we must consider it to make this book complete. *Millepora,* the fire coral belongs to the order **Hydrocorallia** of the class **Hydrairia.**

Despite its distant relationship to the **Madrepores**

the magnificent golden-coloured colony of *Millepora* looks very like the stony corals in its overall appearance. Only the details of embryology, anatomy and histology reveal the true relationships of the fire coral. There is a medusoid stage in the life-cycle which is never found in the **Anthozoa,** the calcareous skeleton has no septa, and there are gastrophores, or feeding polyps ; dactylophores, or defensive polyps, which are reduced to a bunch of long tentacles with batteries of powerful nematocysts ; and gonophores, or reproductive polyps.

Ahermatypic corals, the corals of the deep sea

In parallel with the classification of corals by relationship, which we have already detailed, corals can also be classified by ecology into two distinct types. These are Hermatypic corals, whose cells contain zooxanthellae and which are responsible for the construction of coral reefs in tropical seas, and Ahermatypic corals, which have no zooxanthellae, and do not form coral reefs.

This second group live mostly in very deep water, and are therefore comparatively little studied. They are the opposite in many ways to their relatives which build reefs. Apart from sharing a dislike of low salinities, the effects of all other environmental conditions seem to be reversed in these corals. They can live in all temperatures, even at depths in the polar seas, they are neither dazzled by strong light near the surface nor afraid of the eternal darkness of the abyss. (The actual depht record is held by *Fungicyathus,* dredged from 6,000 metres). They can tolerate water low in dissolved oxygen, as is often the case in the slowly renewed water of the ocean depths. Surprisingly, despite the difficult conditions imposed on animals living at these abyssal depths, all of the classes of cnidaria which we have considered have ahermatypic forms, which are adapted to this life in the abyss.

The adaptations of physiology and of the generic information carried by these corals are all related to their common lack of zooxanthellae.

The vital role of these algae in the reef-building corals is emphasized by the differences found in their deep-water relatives.

It is well known that reef building corals grow more and more slowly, and eventually die, if kept in the dark, even if they are well-fed with planktonic food. How then, can the ahermatypic corals, which have descended from common ancestors to the reef-building corals, and are often classified in the same order or even the same genus, dispense with this symbiosis ? How can they obtain the balance of sugars necessary for their growth and skeletal construction ?

Certainly these ahermatypic corals grow very slowly compared with reef-building corals, and it is likely that they have made modifications of their enzymes to enable them to use precious protein food as a basis for their carbohydrate needs. Protein is more expensive to manufacture in energy terms, but in the case of ahermatypic corals they have no ready supply of carbohydrates.

The fact that this mechanism is actually less efficient than the possession of zooxanthellae is proven by the fact that these deep-water corals grow extremely slowly, their growth to a particular size takes centuries rather than decades. However in the abyss the pace of time is different, and these corals have constructed great reefs, only recently discovered by photographic means, in the perietual calm of the depths.

Reefs and Atolls, the coral communities

We must now consider the corals on a completely different scale. The point of interest in this chapter will be not the polyp but the entire colony, which can itself be considered as though it were a cell within an entire organ, the coral reef.

The conditions required for construction and survival of the reef (of hermatypic corals) are very precise in terms of temperature, salinity, water clarity, illumination and oxygenation.

Corals are very sensitive to cold. They are happiest in water of 25° C to 29° C and will only tolerate a few degrees less than this. Below 18° C they categorically refuse to grow, and at this temperature they will not born reefs. It is this temperature requirement that explains why corals only thrive between the latitudes of 32° N and 30° S. This sensitivity to cold also explains the absence of coral reefs on the Pacific coast of South America where the cold Humboldt current flows, and along the Atlantic coast of Africa which is washed by the Benguela current of Antartic water.

A reef channel connecting the lagoon to the open sea on the island of Moorea in French Polynesia. In the background the ocean waves break over the edge of the reef which is covered with corals and calcareous algae, while in the foreground most of the bottom is covered by sand.

Corals also need water of high salinity, at least 35 parts per thousand of sodium chloride, and they prefer water of 40 parts per thousand salinity, such as occurs in the Red Sea. This prevents corals from growing in regions such as the estuaries of large rivers, where a large input of fresh water dilutes the sea. Hence the absence of corals from the region around the Amazon delta, the Indus and the Ganges. Heavy rainfall for long periods can also dilute the surface waters in lagoons and on reef flats, and may affect some species.

Coral requires very clear water, and cannot survive in even slightly turbid conditions. This is another reason for its absence in the vicinity of rivers, which always produce silty water. Vast amounts of soil and mud may be carried by this freshwater for thousands of kilometres and may prevent growth of coral even if the salinity is suitable.

Within a few square metres of sea bed five or six different genera of corals are each defending their territory. The growth of one may hinder the expansion of the others and is therefore a form of competition.

The reason for this love of clear water is that coral loves sunlight. The sun's rays are rapidly absorbed even by clear water, and the need for light for photosynthesis by the zooxanthellae prevents vigorous coral growth below 50 metres. A few species can survive slightly below this depth by careful utilisation of the light available.

Finally corals require water rich in oxygen. Their respiration and various metabolic activities consume great amounts of dissolved oxygen, though some of this may be supplied by photosynthesis from the zooxanthellae, as the process produces oxygen from carbon dioxide. If all these environmental conditions are met coral can flourish, and the beautiful reefs will be able to grow. Reefs can be classified as several types, all of which grow upwards from several dozen metres to just reach the surface and be exposed slightly at low tide. The four main types of reef are determined mainly by the type of support or base from which they grow and their subsequent modification of that base.

The fringing reef grows at the edge of a continent or island and follows the coastline beneath the water.

The barrier reef is created when a fringing reef becomes separated from its original coastline by a gradual rise in sea level or sinking of the land mass. This sinking must be gradual so that the reef can extend upwards, without being submerged too deeply for coral growth.

Encased within an imposing wall of Porites *the giant clams (*Tridacna*) betray their presence by their superbly coloured mantles. Other bivalves are ensuring their own safety by living within the colony in the foreground.*

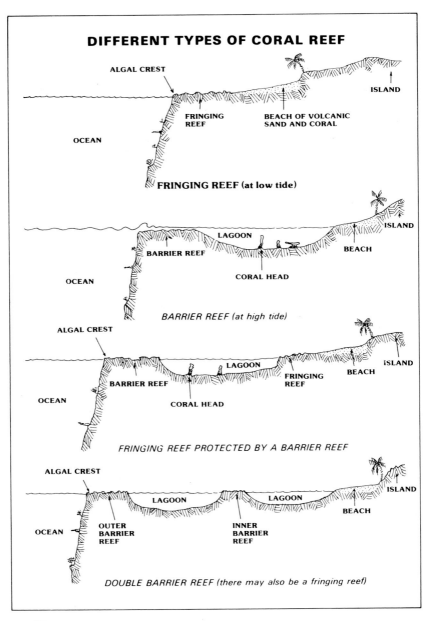

DIFFERENT TYPES OF CORAL REEF

FRINGING REEF (at low tide)

BARRIER REEF (at high tide)

FRINGING REEF PROTECTED BY A BARRIER REEF

DOUBLE BARRIER REEF (there may also be a fringing reef)

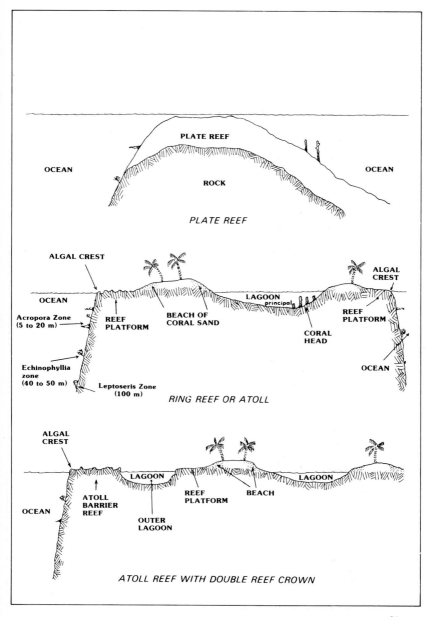

PLATE REEF

RING REEF OR ATOLL

ATOLL REEF WITH DOUBLE REEF CROWN

These first two reef types may occur alone or be associated together. Barrier reefs are generally similar in character but fringing reefs vary in morphology according to whether or not they are protected by a barrier reef. Without this protection the fringing reef is subjected to oceanic swell and therefore takes on many of the characteristics of a barrier reef. In some parts of the world there are double barrier reefs, and in this case the inner one is more like a protected fringing reef, for the same reasons.

The plate reef is often encountered among the formations of the Great Barrier Reef of Australia. It grows on shelves of shallow water regions and is often elongated and called a ribbon reef.

The ring reef or Atoll is a special case of a fringing reef where the island which it surrounded has gradually sunk beneath the surface, leaving only the upgrowing ring of living coral rock. In the centre a lagoon is formed and the reef is usually breached by tidal action to give connecting channels from lagoon to open sea. In a few cases successive subsidences have formed first an encircling barrier reef, with a fringing reef growing inside it, and finally a double ring reef. This occurs in the Caroline Islands for example.

The arrangement of coral species of different colonial form is very characteristic in these various types of reefs. Both vertical and horizontal zonations can be distinguished and these are modified by a variety of factors. The horizontal zonation is primarily controlled by the direction of the prevailing winds, and hence the prevailing swell. No matter what the reef type the portion facing the prevailling winds must stand up to constant battering and pounding by the swell. Only the most sturdy coral colonies, such as members of the **Faviinae,** can stand up to this treatment. In contrast, the side away from the prevailing wind is relatively calm, and supports a far greater variety of species. The quietest waters of all are inside the lagoon, behind the protection of the reef front, and it is here that horizontal zonation is most obvious. Often however there seems to be no rhyme nor reason for the distribution of various species in the lagoon. Great plains of stagshorn coral *(Acropora cervicornis)* may give way in places to dense stands of gorgonians while elsewhere crowds of massive *Porites* or battlements of *Meandrina* may dominate the scene. This confusion does in fact usually indicate certain conditions, and may not be as random as it appears.

As for vertical distribution, this can best be seen where a barrier reef drops off in a sheer vertical cliff-face. The border is protected by vigorous growth of the calcareous algae which cement the reef together, but at a depth of four or five metres where the strenght of the waves is somewhat reduced, many species of *Acropora* and *Pocillopora* appear, along with areas of *Porites* and strong barriers of *Millepora.* The tree-like forms adapt themselves to various degrees of calmness of the water, their strong short branches give way to fine graceful branches at slightly greater depths. In these conditions the clarity of the water permits maximum penetration of the sunlight and with the high oxygenation of the water caused by the incessant turbulence of the swell, an unsurpassed luxuriance of the coral colonies is produced. Below twenty metres other genera appear, such as *Echinophyllia,* while the *Acropora* become less abundant.

This double horizontal and vertical zonation is further modified by latitude, mainly due to the effect of water temperature. The Australian Great Barrier reef provides a particularly good example of this influence. This reef stretches for 2,910 kilometres in a North-west to

South-easterly direction, between the latitudes of 10° and 24° south. Given this huge reef exposed to similar conditions but with a temperature range it is easy to determine the effects of temperature as the major variable. Some species grow markedly better in the warmer waters, and moreover the size of individual colonies directly affects the size of the reef as a whole, the larger the colonies the more extensive the reef.

Finally we must look at the growth patterns of the coral community, which means essentially examining the growth rates and patterns of the polyps themselves. There are no general rules, each genus and even each species has its own particular growth rate, and this may be modified by local environmental conditions. To generalise we can say that massive forms only increase by a few millimetres a year while the treelike branching colonies may grow by several centimetres in the same period. To gain an idea of the actual growth rates we can cite a few well-authenticated examples : 1 — Saville Kent observed a colony of *Porites* in 1890 when its diameter was 5.8 metres. Twenty years later the same colony had reached 7 metres. 2 — In 1857 an *Acropora* 5 metres tall was found growing on a wreck which had sunk 65 years previously, in 1792. 3 — Two years after the eruption of Krakatoa corals 10 centimetres high were found growing on the newly formed rock.

The growth rate of colonies is not steady, however, and decreases considerably as the colony ages. It also seems likely that, as in all animals and plants, the polyps eventually become senile and all growth ceases. This age cannot be measured in decades, but in centuries, and is difficult for a short-lived creature such as ourselves to determine.

The history of the earth as told by the corals

All of this chapter is based on the fundamental discovery that fossil corals of the quaternary period are virtually identical to those living today. From this fact we can make a number of deductions about events in the earth's history since the quaternary age.

The most simple deductions concern the movement of the earth's crust. Knowing that reef corals cannot live below fifty metres, the discovery of their remains at greater depths proves that the sea bed must have sunk, while alternatively their appearance in mountains high above sea level indicates a raising of the earth's crust. For instance, on the island of Makatea in the Tuamotu Archipelago, the coral cliffs extend to a height of forty-five metres above sea level, showing that Makatea represents an ancient reef whose cliffs once formed the dropoff at the edge of the reef. Similar phenomena have been discovered at other places in the world by geologists. There are examples of lowering of the sea level, which brings about a similar appearance of a once-submerged reef into the open air. Such studies have revealed a lowering of sea level by 1.80 metres which must have occurred within the last 6000 years.

Further deductions about past conditions can be made by studying the form of certain species. *Acropora* for instance, shapes its colonies according to the currents, and the rhythm and direction of the swell. Study of the fossil remains of other species, which show a series of concentric annual growth rings when sectioned, just like a tree trunk, can reveal a great deal. Not only are these growth rings precise to the year, but on a finer scale even days can be resolved. A point not brought out when we discussed the building of the skeleton now becomes very important. Growth of the

skeleton occurs mainly during the daytime, it is much reduced, with the physical and chemical reactions which produce the organic material almost ceasing, at night. At the microscopic level this results in a series of minute lamellae being laid down, each of which represents one days work by the polyp. The fine scale of these lines can be understood when it is realised that two or three centimetres of annual growth must contain 365 of these lamellae. This is only of academic interest until it is realised that a series of larger scale patterns in these lamellae can also be seen, and these correspond with the phases of the moon, the distance

A « micro-atoll ». The upper layer of this coral platform is dead, asphyxiated and dehydrated by a drop in sea level. Coral growth can only occur on the areas which are totally immersed. This platform shows, on a small scale, how an atoll is formed.

between one set of most prominent rings and the next being one lunar cycle. The existence of this precisely synchronised and highly accurate calendar in a whole series of fossil corals is very useful to specialists in a variety of fields. The most keenly interested have been the astronomers and geophysicists, who believed that the earth's speed of rotation was gradually slowing down, on the basis of other evidence and theoretical calculations. This slowing should have resulted in an increase in the length of a day of two seconds in a period of one hundred thousand years and also in a gradual increase of the distance between the earth and the moon. An American researcher, MacDonald, concluded from his calculations that the length of a day in Cambrian times would have been twenty-one hours and that therefore there would have been four hundred and twenty days in each year. Imagine his delight when biologists discovered that six hundred million year old corals of the Cambrian period had four hundred and twenty four layers corresponding to one years growth ! In the Silurian era, four hundred million years ago, there are only four hundred layers per year in the corals, and the numbers continue to decrease until we reach those of the present day, which have three hundred and sixty five layers.

Corals and Man

Although modest the place of corals in the affairs of man cannot be completely neglected. They are notorious for their part in many sea dramas of the days of sailing ships. One reef was named the Silver Bank, because of the fact that over fifty Spanish Galleons loaded with silver treasure from central America foundered there and now lie in several metres of water. Over five hundred ships have fallen victim to the Great Barrier Reef of Australia since it was discovered by Captain Cook, who damaged his own ship on it in 1770. As if to hide these misdeeds the coral rapidly covers its victims with new colonies and consumes them forever into its continuously expanding reef structure.

Corals do not only affect man adversely, by ambushing his ships. Both today and from ancient time their beauty has resulted in them being used for decorative purposes. All around the Mediterranean archaeologists have discovered pieces of jewellery in which the red coral takes pride of place. In the period 400 B.C. to 50 B.C. *Corallium rubrum* was frequently used to decorate bracelets, buckles, helmets and even ceremonial harnesses for horses.

During the 15th and 16th centuries, when the early navigators were discovering the reefs of the Antilles and the Indian Ocean, other types of coral were frequently used alongside precious stones in pieces of jewellery. Even so, Europe lagged far behind China and Japan, where the art of polishing and working coral had been known for a long time. It is only the skeleton of the polyps which is used, and it is worked in a similar way to Ivory. Collecting and fashioning coral in this way is still a flourishing industry in Japan and Italy.

The rarity of coral in olden times was such that it was used as a form of currency in Tibet in the 18th century. As recently as the 19th century corals were believed to have magical and medicinal properties in Europe. They were used in necklaces, earings and amulets, and have even been attributed curative properties when applied in powdered form. Even today Arab craftsmen on the shores of the Red Sea carve necklaces from black coral and attribute mysterious powers to them.

Coral can also contribute to public works. In the Maldives Atolls there is such a shortage of rock as a building material that coral is used instead. This badly disfigures the coral shores and decimates their fauna. Recently the natives of the Maldives have built many houses and jetties from small coral bricks which are quarried fro the shores with explosives.

But to most people the true home of the corals is beneath the sea. Cinema and television have played a large part in spreading the knowledge and love of the fabulous coral world to places far removed from the tropics. To see it at first hand, however, it is important to exercise some caution. If you wish to collect a specimen then you should wear strong gloves. Take care if snorkelling or diving to wear protective clothing, and do not let the swell knock you against the reef. When walking across the reef always wear old but strong shoes. The slightest cut or graze from coral can become seriously inflamed and infected. This does not always happen, simple contact with most corals, especially if diving during the daytime when most of the polyps are retracted, causes no harmful or painful sensations except in the case of one or two species, for instance *Millepora*. Even with this species the sting is no more painful than that of the common stinging nettle. The same cannot be said of superficial grazes or clean cuts, where the intensity of the inflammation is out of all proportion with the size of the cut. The affected region becomes painfully inflamed and somewhat incapacitated. Festering is rare but the area affected may spread, developing into a type of sore, especially at certain times of the year. The inhabitants of the Tuamotu islands, the Paumotu, know this phenomenon well and talk of the Southern spring as being the time of year when the coral « flowers ». At this time the coral sores are most serious, and develop slowly in a manner quite unlike their behaviour during the rest of the year. It seems that during this period the corals produce a toxic substance different to the nematocyst poison. This substance has not yet been isolated, but must have some necrotic property as these sores tend to get bigger, sometimes becoming vast ulcerations with little tendency to heal. Surprisingly, small cuts from fish that live amongst the coral show the same development at this time of the year, as though the poison from the coral has been transferred to their skins. During the rest of the year most coral sores are merely painful and incapacitating, but heal quickly with simple medical treatment or even by the cures of the local inhabitants such as the use of lime juice as an antiseptic.

To conclude it may be useful to give some advice to those who wish. to collect small souvenirs of the coral itself, rather than the preferable ones of photographs or films.

Collection of coral has already caused considerable damage to some areas of reefs. In some parts of the world Underwater parks with very strict rules of no collecting are being established to prevent this sort of vandalism.

Firstly, then, there must be no more of this wanton destruction. Obviously it is pointless to break off a great, fifty year old, head of *Acropora* when only a small piece will be actually kept. Like eveything else, corals obey Archimedes principle. A large branch of coral weighs very little in water, but when removed from the water it becomes so heavy that it will break under its own weight, or at least become so fragile that to transport it is out of the question. A small hacksaw or a diving knife will easily remove the coveted specimen without any damage to the whole colony.

The real problems only begin when the coral is removed from the water. After, only a few hours the corals will begin to give off a foul smell, which is totally impossible to live with. To avoid this, or at least reduce it to a tolerable level, the coral polyps must be killed

Top plate : Coral boulders on the reef flat make an ideal habitat for many species of sponges, echinoderms and molluscs. All these animals die rapidly if the boulder is upturned by a careless collector ; the lower plate shows the same boulder a few days later.

immediately after collection by placing the specimen in fresh water for about twelve hours. For many species washing with a high pressure jet of water will produce spectacular results in only seconds, the soft parts are torn away and the skeleton rapidly turns white, losing its smell very quickly. For other species this bleaching and deodourising requires the action of sunlight. Recreation of the conditions on the beach of an atoll is what is required. There, coral fragments can be collected which have been broken off by storms and have acquired their desired whiteness by long exposure to the sun and frequent rinsing by the sea.

To attain this desired result takes many days and a lot of patience, as the coral must be turned regularly to allow the sunlight to fall on it from all sides.

When leaving for home the collector has more problems to overcome. In order to prevent his souvenirs arriving home in pieces they must be carefully packed to withstand the battering to which luggage is invariably submitted. At least the more fragile pieces must be packed in rigid cardboard or plastic boxes with a packing of sawdust or rice to act as a shock absorber. On returning home a good bath of diluted bleach for a few hours will give the specimens the immaculate whiteness which they deserve. Each piece about the house will bring back memories of long and pleasant hours spent underwater.

Catalogue of the principal species of coral

The specimens included in this catalogue are listed under their generic and specific names. Where the generic name is followed by « sp ». the specimen in question has been identified to generic level but not to species, (for example *Acropora sp.* signifies a species of the genus *Acropora*). The reader will also find the term « cf ». between the names of some genera and species, indicating that the species name is not certain, but at least a close relative.

The hundred and fifty or so species included here represent the most commonly encountered types of corals, but are a poor reflection of the true diversity of corals when it is considered that there are between two thousand five hundred and two thousand six hundred species in existence today. This figure includes Alcyonaceans and Gorgonaceans which are not regarded as true corals by some experts.

These two thousand five hundred species are the total for the whole world, but never all exist on the same reef. Thus the reefs of the tropical west Atlantic, mainly those of the Antilles, have only about twenty genera and sixty species of corals. The rare coral formations of the west African coast contain only about fifteen species. In contrast, eighty genera and over six hundred species may be found in reef regions of the Indo-Pacific. This is the most extensive coral region, and probably because of this the most luxuriant. Even in the richest regions the spreading out of the genera and species is well marked. For example, in the lagoon of New Caledonia, held to be one of the highlights of the coral world, recent research on the family Faviinae has shown that only thirty four species (belonging to eight genera) are actually present, while one hundred and forty seven species of this family are described in the literature. It is true that there is also an enormous problem with the literature itself, that of synonymies.

To identify many species of coral is in fact a very difficult task. In order to name a newly discovered species and place it in the appropriate genus, or perhaps even create a new genus for it, the minute details of structure of the calyces, of their partitions and septa, the presence or absence of synapticules or walls, the number of cycles of tentacles, etc. must all be studied. With all these characters to be considered it is easy to imagine the misunderstandings that can arise, especially with old descriptions which may lack relevant details. To illustrate the problem of synonymies an example will be useful :
- In 1786 Ellis and Solander described a previously unknown madrepore coral and called it *Madrepora cyathus.*
- In 1801 Lamarck, in his work on the madrepores, created a new genus *Caryophyllia* and from that time *Madrepora cyathus* became the type species of this new genus under the new name, *Caryophyllia cyathus.*
- All this was thrown into confusion when Ehrenberg

MAJOR CORAL REGIONS OF THE WORLD

Distribution of genera and species in the main coral regions :

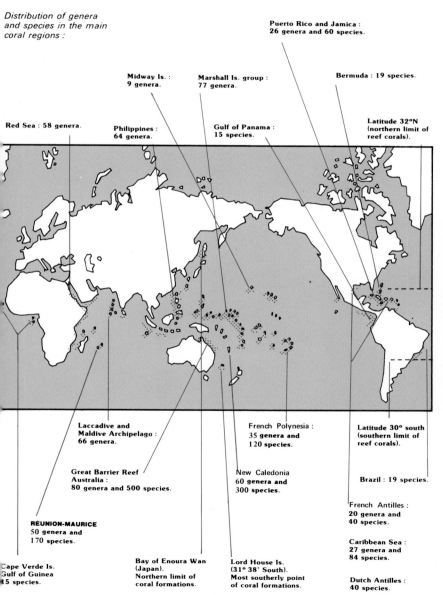

Puerto Rico and Jamica :
26 genera and 60 species.

Midway Is. :
9 genera.

Marshall Is. group :
77 genera.

Bermuda : 19 species.

Red Sea : 58 genera.

Philippines :
64 genera.

Gulf of Panama :
15 species.

Latitude 32°N
(northern limit of
reef corals).

Laccadive and
Maldive Archipelago :
66 genera.

French Polynesia :
35 genera and
120 species.

Latitude 30° south
(southern limit of
reef corals).

Great Barrier Reef
Australia :
80 genera and 500 species.

New Caledonia
60 genera and
300 species.

Brazil : 19 species.

RÉUNION-MAURICE
50 genera and
170 species.

French Antilles :
20 genera and
40 species.

Caribbean Sea :
27 genera and
84 species.

Cape Verde Is.
Gulf of Guinea
15 species.

Bay of Enoura Wan
(Japan).
Northern limit of
coral formations.

Lord House Is.
(31° 38' South).
Most southerly point
of coral formations.

Dutch Antilles :
40 species.

described the peculiarities of a new genus *Cyathina*, in 1834, into which *Caryophyllia cyathus* fits perfectly, becoming then *Cyathina cyathus.*

— In 1857 appeared « L'histoire naturelle des Coralliaires » (the natural history of Corals) by Milne-Edwards, the authority on corals at the time. He reinstated the name *Caryophyllia cyathus* to this species whose name changes we have followed fron 1786. Meanwhile, however this same species had been called *Galatea cyathus* by Oken in 1815, then *Anthophyllum cyathus* by Schweigger in 1820. Milne-Edwards opinion was accepted until Seguenza in 1863 came to decide that this species belonged to a new genus ; *Ceratocyathus...* !

Luckily not all species of coral have suffered this same fluctuation of names, most of which are unnecessary changes. Today there are a set of rules to minimise the changing of names by zoologists, though refinement of our knowledge of relationships may still necessitate some changes. The species which are shown in the colour plates here have been given their currently accepted names, and will serve to enable identification when on the next submarine excursion, giving a greater interest and value to any observations.

Two divers swim in the blue water of the reef. In the apparent monotony of this vast area of Montipora *their eye area skinned to pick out the detail which is invisible in a photograph. On the following pages the reader will be able to discover this detail for himself.*

Principal types of coral

CLASS HEXACORALLIA

ACROPORIDAE

Plates 1 to 3 : **Acropora sp.**

The family **Acroporidae** consists of the many types of coral which possess a branching bushlike form of growth, as illustrated in the following pages. They provide an ideal refuge for a complete fauna of invertebrates and small fishes, particularly **Chromis** and **Dascyllus**.

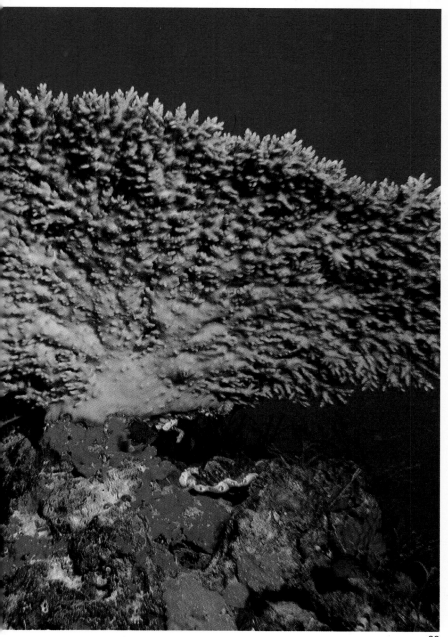

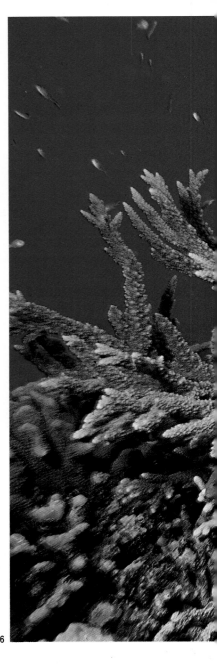

Plates 4 to 6 : **_Acropora sp._**

No matter where on the reef the **Acropora** colonies are situated they always try to expose the maximum of their surface area to the light. Thus the colony in plate 4 is spreading out horizontally although it is attached to a vertical face of the reef. Also the fineness of the branches and whether they are soldered together at their bases depends on the turbulence of the water.

6

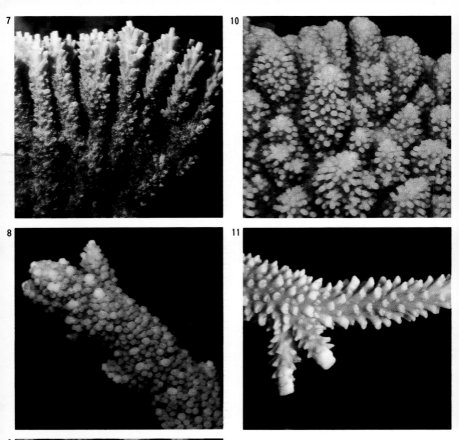

Plates 7 to 12 : **Acropora sp.**

The degree of polymorphism within the family **Acroporidae** is remarkable. By careful examination using a binocular microscope it is possible to determine the species of a particular specimen. The extensive use of the epithet sp. indicates our ignorance of which species are actually represented in these photographs.

Plate 12 : taken at night, shows the extended tentacles of the polyps which wave in the water currents collecting zooplankton.

*Plate 13 (previous page) : **Acropora palmata.***

*This is the most massive species of **Acropora**. It prefers to live just below the surface and is found mainly in the Caribbean.*

*Plates 14 to 16 : **Acropora sp.***

*Plate 17 : **Acropora cf palifera***

*Plate 18 : **Acropora sp.***

*Plate 19 : **Acropora cervicornis***

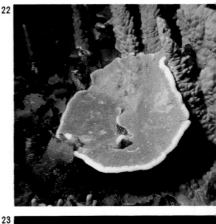

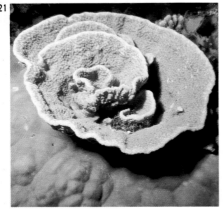

Plate 20 : **Acropora sp.**
Plate 21 : **Montipora cf verrilli**
Plate 22 : **Montipora sp.**
Plate 23 : Skeleton of **Montipora sp.**
Without its solft parts and after the removal of the incrustations of algae, the coral takes on the whiteness of the calcium carbonate from which it is constructed. The photograph of the **Montipora sp.** opposite (plate 24 illustrates the normal colours of the colonies « in situ ». Plate 25, following page : **Montipora sp.** expanding its « Petals » like a gigantic flower to collect the rays of sunlight.

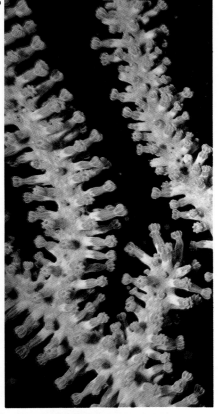

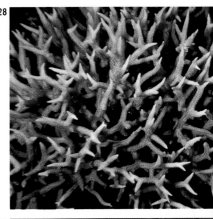

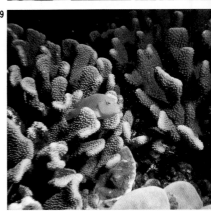

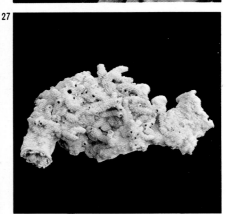

SERIATOPORIDAE
Plate 26 : **Madracis sp.**
Plate 28 : **Seriatopora hytrix**
Plate 30 : **Seriatopora sp.**

ASTROCOENIIDAE
Plate 27 : Skeleton of **Stylocoeniella sp.**, the only genus of the family **Astrocoeniidae** represented in the book.

POCILLOPORIDAE
PLate 29 and plate 30 on the following page : **Pocillopora sp.**

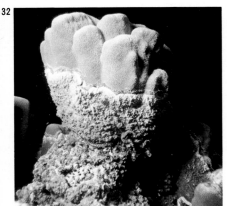

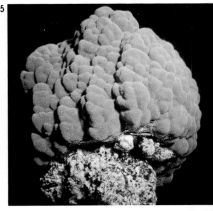

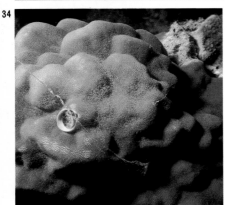

PORITIDAE

*Plates 32, 34, 37 : **Porites sp.***
*Plate 33 : **Porites cf lobata**.*
The **Porites** construct massive colonies in which each polyp inhabits only a minute calyx. Many molluscs find shelter by attaching themselves to this type of colony. (Plates 34 and 37).
Plate 38, following page : A large pyramidal colony of **Porites sp.** forming an umbrella for the coral fishes.

39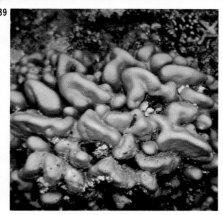

42

40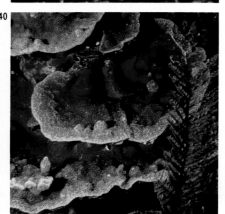

43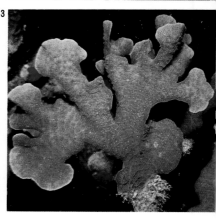

41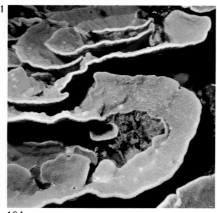

Plate 39 : **Porites sp.**
Plate 40 and 41 : **Synaraea sp. :**
these two species of the family **Poritii-**
dae *have colonies made up of lamellae
rather like the family* **Agariciidae**
which follows.
Plate 42. **Goniopora sp. :** *the polyps
of this species are very long when
extended.*

AGARICIIDAE
Plate 43 : **Agaricia agaricites**
Plate 44 : **Agaricia sp.**

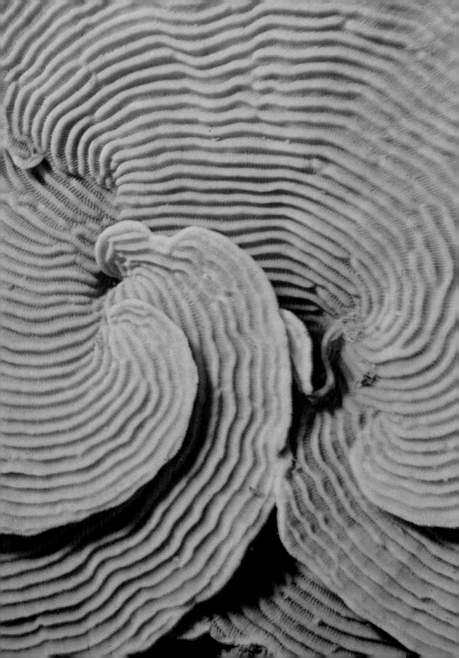

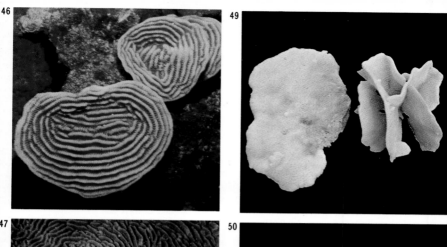

47

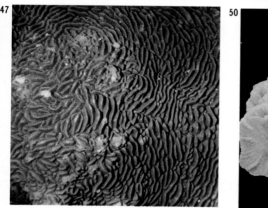

50

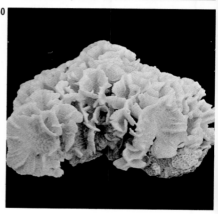

48

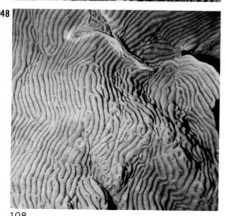

Plate 45 previous page : **Pachyseris speciosa** *which somewhat resembles a gastropod shell with its sculpture of fine enrolled lines.*

Plates 46 to 49 and 51 : **Pachyseris sp.** *(note that the two specimens in plate 49 are skeletal preparations indicated by their whiteness.)*

Plate 50 : Skeleton of **Pavona cf. frondifera,** *which also belongs to the family* **Agariciidae.**

Plate 52 : **Pavona cactus**

THAMNASTRAEIDAE
Plate 53 : **Psammocora sp. :** our only representative of this family.

FUNGIIDAE
Plate 54 : **Fungia fungites**
Plate 55 : the same species surrounded by a crescent of **Herpolitha limax**.
Plate 56 : following page : one of natures mistakes. This « monster » of the family **Fungiidae** which resembles a four-armed starfish is a **Fungia**. This specimen has been turned over to reveal the underside.

EUPSAMMIIDAE
Plate 57 : **Coenopsammia aurea**
Plate 58 : Skeleton of **Turbinaria sp.**
Plate 60 : **Coenopsammia sp.**

DENDROPHYLLIIDAE
plate 59 : Skeleton of **Dendrophyllia nigrescens**
Plate 61 : **Dendrophyllia sp.**
These two coral families usually possess a tubular calyx with the soft polyp occupying only the outermost tips.

62

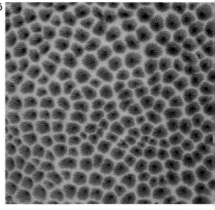

65

63

66

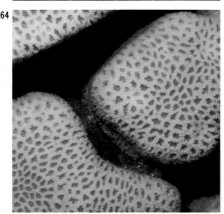

64

FAVIIDAE

Plates 62 to 64 and plates 66 and 67 :
Favia sp.
Plate 65 : **Leptastrea sp.**

The family **Faviidae** *rivals that of the* **Acroporidae** *for the largest number of species. In the six species shown on these pages the calyces of each individual are separate structures. It is shown on the following pages, that in other species of this family this is not always the case, and that skeletal morphology can vary greatly even within the same family.*

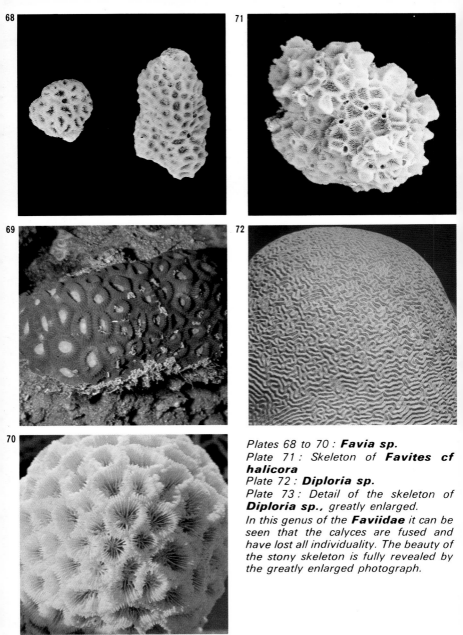

Plates 68 to 70 : **Favia sp.**
Plate 71 : Skeleton of **Favites cf halicora**
Plate 72 : **Diploria sp.**
Plate 73 : Detail of the skeleton of **Diploria sp.,** greatly enlarged.
In this genus of the **Faviidae** it can be seen that the calyces are fused and have lost all individuality. The beauty of the stony skeleton is fully revealed by the greatly enlarged photograph.

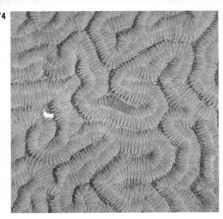

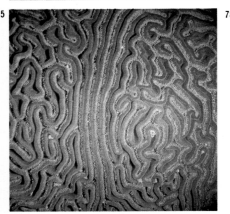

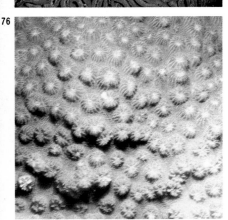

Plate 74 : **Diploria sp.**
Plate 75 : **Diploria labyrinthiformis.**
Plate 76 : **Echinopora sp.**
Plate 77 : **Colpophyllia sp.**
Plate 78 : **Cladocora cœspitosa,**
this is one of the three **Hexacorallia,**
obviously non-reef-building types,
which may be encountered by a diver
in the Mediterranean, though only at
several metres from the surface.

MUSSIDAE
Plate 79 : **Platygyra sp.**

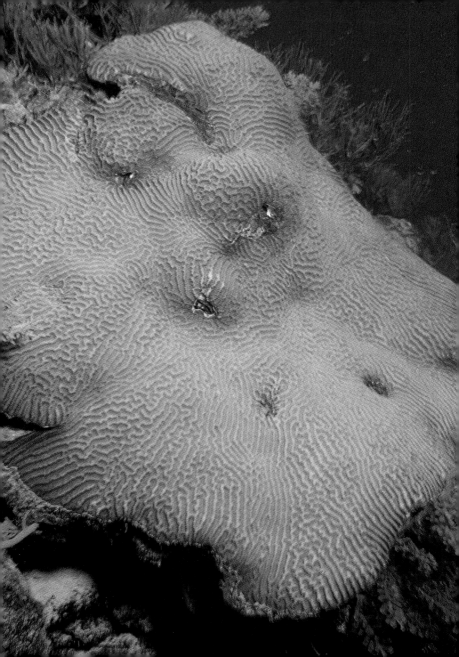

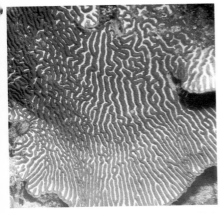

83

84

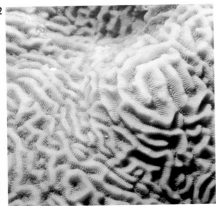

82

Plates 80 to 82 : **Platygyra sp.**
Plates 83 : two skeletal preparations of **Platygyra sp.**

Plate 84 : – top and bottom left : two skeletal preparations of **Platygyra cf sinenois ;** – bottom right : **Leptoria sp.**

In these types the calyces and polyps are fused into long series of ridges, winding to various degrees in different species.

Plate 85 : **Lobophyllia corymbosa,** another genus of the **Mussidae** in which the calyces are very large and well isolated from each other.

Plate 86 : Skeleton of **Lobophyllia costata.**

Plate 87 : **Favia sp. (FAVIIDAE)**

Plate 88 : The extended soft parts with their spreading tentacles hides the calyces of this coral. The genus of this coral is not known. If the tentacles are counted it can be seen that there are always twelve, a multiple of six, and therefore it must belong to the **Hexacorallia.**

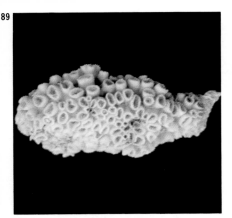

MONTASTREIDAE

Plate 89 : Skeleton of **Montastrea sp.**

Plate 90 : **Montastrea curta.** Here also the tentacles are extended but they are so fine and short that they do not hide the calyces. They merely form short tufts to which a number of predators are very partial.

MEANDRINIDAE

Plate 91 : Skeleton of **Meandrina sp.** Found virtually only in the Caribbean, this is the classic « Neptune's Brain ».

91

Plate 92 : **Meandrina sp.**

MERULINIDAE
Plate 93 : Skeleton of **Merulina ampliata**

OCULINIDAE
Plate 94 : **Galaxea cf explanata.**

In the genus **Galaxea** the mineral lace-work of the calyx reaches the limits of fineness and fragility. Each of these septa is covered by a thin layer of soft tissue and becomes greatly drawn out to form a crown-like struture.

94

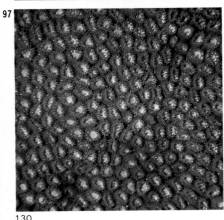

Plate 95 : **Turbinaria sp. (EUP-SAMMIIDAE)**
Plate 96 : **Favia sp. (FAVIIDAE)**
Plate 97 : **Solenastrea sp. (FAVII-DAE)**
Plate 98 : **Astrangia sp. (ASTRA-GIIDAE)**
Plate 99 : **Galaxea fascicularis (OCULINIDAE)**
Skeleton seen in profile.

Plate 100 : **Cyphastrea sp. (FA-VIIDAE)**
Plate 101 following page : **Pectinia lactuca (PECTINIIDAE)**. Detail of the skeleton greatly magnified.

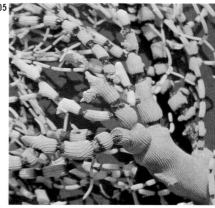

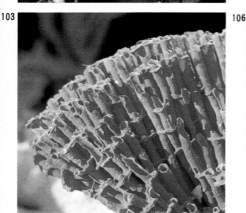

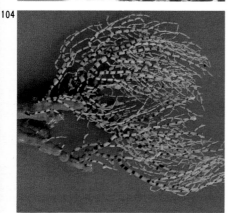

CLASS OCTOCORALLIA

Plate 102 : **Corallium rubrum (CO-RALLIDA)**
At night it uses its eight tentacles to collect zooplankton.

Plate 103 : Skeleton of **Tubipora musica**, the organpipe coral **(STO-LONIFERA)**

Plate 104 and 105 : Skeleton of **Isis hippuris (GORGONACEA)**
Note the horny nodes and calcareous internodes of this last species shown enlarged in plate 105. This structure makes the skeleton very fragile.

108

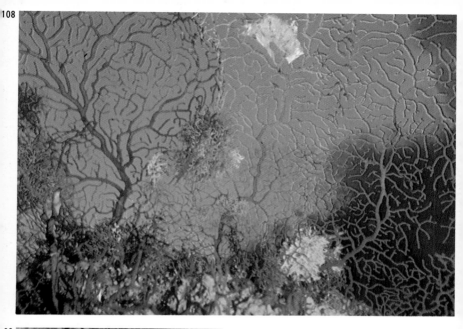

09

10

Plate 106 : **Eunicella cavolini (GORGONACEA)**
Plate 107 : **Sarcophyton sp. (AL-CYONACEA)**
Plate 108 : **Paramuricea clavata (GORGONACEA)**
Plate 109 : **Palythoa sp.** (colonial **ZOANTHID)**
Plate 110 and 111 : **Sarcophyton sp.**
The **Alcyonaceans** and colonial **Zoanthids** are both called soft corals because of their rubbery texture which is a result of the possession of a skeleton of isolated calcareous spicules. They often colonise considerable areas of reef flats.

1

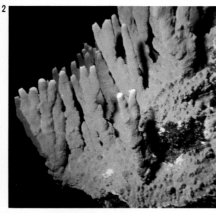

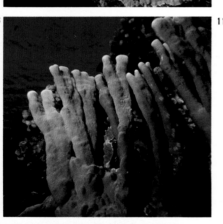

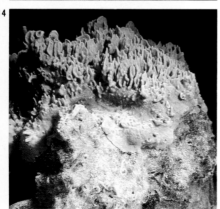

CLASS HYDRAIRIA

Plate 112 to 114 **Millepora sp.**
Plate 115 : **Millepora alcicornis**
Plate 116 and 117 : **Millepora sp.**

Millepora belongs to the order **Hydrocorallia.** The sting of their cnidoblasts is very powerful and contact with them produces a painful burning sensation, therefore these species are given the common name fire coral.

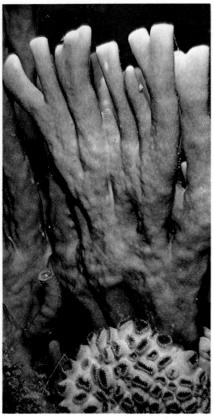

Plate 118 : **Millepora sp.** (a colonial **Zoanthid** of the genus **Palythoa** is growing at the base of the colony).

Plate 119 : A typical example of the struggle for living space between different members of the reef fauna. Surrounding a red sponge are :
− a small tuft of **Acropora sp. ;**
− a disc of **Platygyra sp. ;**
− some sheets of **Cyphastrea sp.** (green).

119

Index of Scientific names

Nature Series
Scientific Editor: Bernard SALVAT

In the same series:

Polynesia:
Plants and Flowers of Tahiti
Birds of Tahiti
An Underwater Guide to Tahiti
Shells of Tahiti
Sharks of Polynesia

Plants and Flowers of Hawai'i
An Underwater Guide to Hawai'i
Shells of Hawai'i
Coral Reefs Fishes of Hawai'i

Melanesia:
Plants and Flowers of New Caledonia
An Underwater Guide to New Caledonia

Caribbean:
Plants and Flowers of the Caribbean
Butterflies and Insects of the Caribbean
Shells of the Caribbean
Underwater guide to the Caribbean

Indian Ocean:
Plants and Flowers of Reunion and Mauritius
Underwater guide to Reunion and Mauritius

South-east Asia:
Birds of Singapore
Plants and Flowers of Singapore

Maquette: Thierry STEFF

Printed in Malaysia
January 1997
Publisher's number: 372